Backyard Biology

Nature Stories and Nature Activities
from My Back Yard and Beyond

Don Salvatore

Illustrations by

Deborah Sovinee

Backyard Biology Books

Backyard Biology Books
56 Ingham Way
Pembroke, MA 02359
781 826-2741

To my wife Louise who shares my love of nature and who has encouraged me to keep writing these stories.
≈Don Salvatore

To my husband George, who understands the importance of messiness to the creative process, and my daughter Chloe who long ago showed me the fascination of dead things found in the street.
≈Deborah Sovinee

Special thanks to :

Doug Lowry for the Catfish Logo

Lynn Baum for the edits

Nature Stories

from My Backyard and Beyond

Table of Contents

Nature Activities

from My Backyard and Beyond

Table of Contents

Introduction

In 1993 I was involved in a macroinvertebrate study for my local watershed association - the North and South Rivers Watershed in southeastern MA. Macroinvertebrates are animals without backbones (invertebrates) that are large enough to see without a microscope (macro). The community of macroinvertebrates in a river is a good indication of its health. Certain macroinvertebrates, like mayflies, caddisflies and stoneflies may indicate clean water while others like midge and blackfly larvae may indicate polluted water. By collecting the macroinvertebrates in a river and identifying them, one can get a picture of the health of the river.

To collect the macroinvertebrates, we would locate a riffle area - a place where the water is no more than a couple of feet deep and moves quickly over rocks. In a riffle area, the macroinvertebrates would be living under the rocks, out of the main force of the river. One member of our team would hold a net on the river bottom just downstream of the rocks. The other member would lift a rock off the bottom and scrub it with a brush, dislodging any organisms attached to the rock. The organisms would be carried by the water into the net. Our catch was placed in a bucket, carried back to the lab and identified.

The variety of life occurring in the riffle areas of the river was impressive. As well as the organisms listed above, we collected dragonflies, damselflies, water pennies, fishflies, hellgrammites, alderflies, crane flies, water beetles, moth larvae, clams, snails, crayfish, eels and more.

The two thousand members of the watershed support the organization both financially and spiritually. They are the stewards of the river and care about its health. They live by the river, walk along the river, fish and boat in the river, and swim in the river. However, most of them have little idea what lives in the river, the very creatures they are protecting by supporting the watershed. Being a longtime science educator, I thought they might be interested in learning about some of these creatures. So I started to write short stories for the Watershed's quarterly newsletter. Each issue would feature one of the animals we collected in our macroinvertebrate study.

Through my writing, I came to realize that all living organisms have a tale to tell. There is no such thing as a boring plant or animal. All I needed to do was look closely and I could find stories just as fascinating in my backyard or

1

at the seashore close to my house. This is how the backyard biology stories came about.

Of course, the creatures I find in my backyard don't give up their stories easily. Sometimes it takes years of scientific investigation to tease out these stories. Most of what we know of nature comes from scientific investigations. Scientists publish their findings in scientific journals. By doing a little research, naturalists are able to piece together the life history of the organism in which they are interested. For instance, after I became curious about the winter firefly, I did an online search and came up with a paper. "Notes on the Life History and Mating Behavior of *Ellychnia corrusca*" by Jennifer Rooney and Sara Lewis at Tufts University. This research was the basis of my nature story, "Chasing Fireflies" (pg. 43).

But science is not just for scientists. We all have a little scientist in us and enjoy finding out how things work. The Nature Activities in this book are a fun, easy way to conduct our very own scientific studies in our back yards. They include simple experiments that can be done using materials found around the house, as well as instructions for making some scientific tools for conducting the experiments.

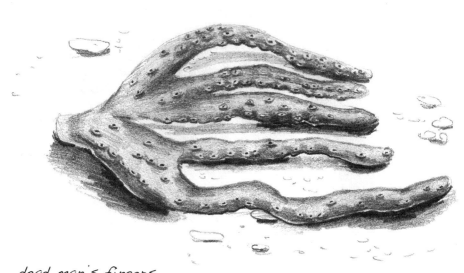

dead man's fingers

The day after a storm is a great
time to walk the beach, looking
for seashore treasures.

1

Seashore Treasures

S tanding on the beach, looking out over the ocean always instills in me a sense of wonder. I wonder what is under the surface. I wonder what strange creatures make the ocean their home. I wonder what they eat, what eats them, what kind of homes they build, how they court and mate. And sometimes I wonder if they are swimming just under the surface wondering about me!

As a long-time scuba diver, I have met and become familiar with many of these sea creatures. Still, it seems that the more I learn, the more there is to wonder about.

For those of you who don't dive, your sense of wonder must be fulfilled by a walk along the beach. The beach is the graveyard of the oceans. Many of the seas' creatures are cast up on the beach after they die. Here you will find the familiar crab shell, the clam or the snail. You will undoubtedly come across many types of algae, the ocean's plants. Fish bones, starfish and sea urchins are all familiar finds to the beachcomber. But occasionally you come across something unfamiliar, something that just makes you wonder. What could it be? Where did it come from? Was it ever alive?

Here are four wonders that you may find on our beaches:

DEAD MAN'S FINGERS   One of the most unusual finds while beachcombing has got to be dead man's fingers. Lying on the beach, they conjure up images of pirates walking the plank, food for the fishes. This creature is actually a type of sponge. Sponges are very simple creatures. They lack most of the body parts that higher organisms are made of. In fact, some sponges have been squeezed through a sieve and the individual cells have actually migrated back together to reform the sponge. If you look closely at the sponge, you will see many small openings and fewer large openings. The small openings are for inhaling water. Inside the sponges' body, the organic material is extracted from the water and the water is then expelled through the larger openings.

The dead man's fingers is a common sponge off our New England coast. They often wash ashore after they die. What you are looking at is just their skeleton; the living part of the sponge is long gone.

Common names for animals can often be confusing. Peterson's Field Guide to the Seashore gives the name of dead man's fingers to a different type of organism, a relative of the corals. But I grew up calling this sponge dead man's fingers and I think it is much more descriptive of the sponge.

SEA WASH BALLS   If you find a cluster of pea sized leathery little pouches about the size of your fist, you have found sea wash balls. Pick it up and shake it. You will hear a rattling sound. What you have found is the egg case of the waved whelk shell. Inside each of the tiny pouches are hundreds of baby snails. Look at the size of the egg mass and consider that the adult snail is from two to four inches long. Makes you wonder, doesn't it!

If you want to know where the name, "sea wash balls" comes from, stick the egg mass in the water and rub it between your hands.

SAND COLLAR   Another egg case that can be commonly found on our beaches is that of the moon snail. A large moon snail might measure four inches across, but its foot is much larger than this. A snail's foot is the fleshy part that the snail glides on. The moon snail's foot secretes large amounts of mucus. It uses this mucus to glue a collar of sand around its body. In this

sand collar are up to 500,000 moon snail eggs. These sand collars are occasionally found washed up on the beaches where moon snails are common. If you pick one up to examine it - be gentle. The dried sand collars are very fragile.

Moon snails leave other evidence of their presence. Look for a clamshell with a perfectly round 1/4 inch beveled hole drilled in it. This clam has been eaten by a moon snail. Moon snails will burrow under the sand, locate a clam and wrap it's foot around it. The moon snail secretes a chemical to soften the shell and then uses its serrated tongue to rasp out the hole through which it devours the clam. I have often wondered how the snail eats the clam through this tiny hole!

MERMAID'S PURSE The find that most typifies a day of beachcombing is the mermaid's purse. This egg case, a black square pouch with curly tentacles at each corner, stands out against the white beach sand. Its occupant was a baby skate. The skate is a type of fish, a close relative of the sharks and stingrays. The curly tentacles are used to catch hold of seaweed and keep the egg case from being cast up on the beach before the skate hatched. Look at the edges of the egg case. If one edge is open, then you know that the skate hatched in time. If the egg case is brown instead of black and no edges are open, then the skate should still be within. Carefully cut open the egg case and if the baby skate is developed enough, it might survive if you place it back in the water.

A day of beachcombing always turns up many surprises. A trip to the library to look up what you have found is a great way to end a day at the beach. But sometimes it is enough just to wonder.

One interesting question I have about a
creature washed up on the beach is:

_____

_____

_____

_____

_____

_____

(All great discoveries start with a question. Ask a question.
Then do some research. Maybe you will find the answer to your
question and maybe you will find the answer to a question you
hadn't asked.)

This space reserved for
Nature Drawings
from my backyard

When they first start singing, spring peepers are impossible to spot. Only after they have been active for a few weeks do they seem to lose their timidity and sing from more exposed perches. Toads, however, do not bother to hide when they sing.

American toad

2

The Frog Basin

When we first looked at the site for the new house, it was an eyesore. A big mud hole taking up almost an acre of land next to where the house would be built. The contractor said that it was for the retention basin, and that it was required by law for a new development so close to the river. All of the water that emptied into the street drains must pass through the basin before flowing into the river. All of the road salt and sand, the leaked antifreeze and oil, the pet droppings and anything else would settle in the basin, leaving only clean water passing into the river. Sounds appealing, doesn't it? Who wouldn't want this pollution sink right next to their brand new house?

After the first year, the basin was looking pretty good. It had filled in with a variety of grasses, rushes and sedges. It was looking pretty wild. In fact, it looked so good that the spring peepers took up abode there. The peeper is our tiniest frog with the loudest voice. Its song is a high pitched rising single note whistle. And it doesn't like to sing alone. Hundreds of males will gather and sing their love songs to the females. But try to find them! At only an inch long and perfectly camouflaged, they are impossible to spot. Yet there is no question they are present. Standing at the edge of the basin, their song is deafening.

After the second year, the cattails colonized the basin. This seemed to agree with the toads, for they soon moved in, adding their voice to that of the peepers. Their song is not as shrill, but just as loud and carries even further than that of the peepers. It is a long trilling whistle and they sing with such gusto that their quivering bodies cause ripples to radiate through the water.

Now in its third year, the wood frogs have taken over one corner of the basin. Wood frogs spend most of their time away from the water - in the woods as their name suggests, but, like all our frogs, they must return to the water to lay their eggs. In fact, they are the first to arrive in the basin. This year, they arrived on March 21. They beat the peepers by one day. The toads were relative latecomers, arriving in early April.

Later in the year, the "summer frogs" will arrive. So far, I have seen green and pickerel frogs in the basin. That still leaves four to make their appearance; the bullfrog, tree frog, leopard frog and fowler's toad.

The appearance of so many frogs in my retention basin indicates to me that the water is very clean. As a group, frogs are very pollution sensitive, and therefore are a good indicator of water quality. Rather than being the pollution trap that I originally thought, the basin is a wonderful addition to the property. It not only cleans the street run-off before entering the river, but in doing so, it has attracted an incredible variety of wildlife in the process.

One interesting question I have about frogs is:

_____

_____

_____

_____

_____

_____

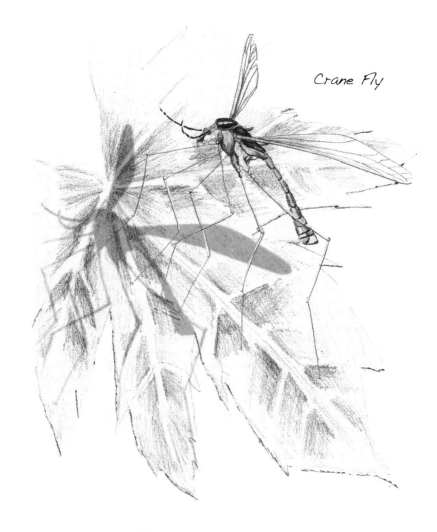

Crane Fly

Like many flying insects, crane
flies are attracted to lights at
night. Look for them around an
outside porch light.

3

The Impostors

Nothing can ruin a summertime picnic quicker than hornets. Childhood memories of the searing pain of a few stings as they protect their nest can send even the most stalwart picnicker fleeing in terror. In vain do we tell ourselves that a wasp (a hornet is a type of wasp) defending her nest is much more likely to sting than a wasp searching for food - even if the food belongs to us. And common sense tells us the bigger the hornet, the bigger the sting. Therefore, a two-inch hornet is an insect to be feared.

A two-inch hornet is most likely a cicada killer, a type of solitary wasp. Unlike hornets, solitary wasps live alone - they are solitary. Their nests consist of a hole dug in the ground. They provision the nest with food, lay an egg, close up the nest then start another. Unlike hornets, they don't care for their young. They are not responsible for the well being of a hive. In fact, once the nest is closed, these wasps pay no more attention to it, intent only on beginning another nest. Having no hive to protect, solitary wasps have little reason to be aggressive.

The Cicada Killer is the largest of our solitary wasps. It provisions its nest with a cicada which it has paralyzed with its sting. The young wasp feeds on the paralyzed cicada. The cicada killer is a gentle, non-aggressive creature (except to the cicada). No one I know has ever been stung by one of these large wasps. That is not to say that it would never sting. But they are certainly no threat to any picnic.

It is a fact of gardening that flowers attract bees. And bees, like wasps, can sting. Still, the joys of a well-tended garden are worth the risk of bothering a few bees. Strangely enough, gardeners and bees tend to get along surprisingly well. Like the hornets, the bees are mostly aggressive around their hive. Even though most gardeners never get stung, they tend to treat all bees with respect.

Flowers attract many insects other than bees, including wasps, butterflies, mosquitoes and flies. One type of fly, the hoverfly, is very noticeable because it looks like a bee. Because it looks like a bee most gardeners treat it with respect. And while all insects should be treated with respect, the hoverfly does not warrant the respect that comes from fear of a sting. The hoverfly can't sting. It is a completely harmless insect. However, just the fact that it looks like a stinging insect affords it protection from its enemies. This type of impersonation is called mimicry. An animal that might not want to take on a bee might be fooled by the hoverfly's looks and leave it alone. Even though the hoverfly has no conscious thought that it looks dangerous, its mimicry works all the same.

There are a couple of ways to tell a hoverfly from a bee. First, it is called a hoverfly because it can hover, staying perfectly still in mid air. Bees can not. Second, all types of bees (as well as wasps) have two pair of wings. All types of flies have only one pair of wings. Count the wings and watch how it flies to know if it stings.

While walking through the woods of a summer evening swatting at a viscous swarm of mosquitoes, who has not wondered if it were possible for mosquitoes to suck a human dry. With that thought in mind, imagine spotting the granddaddy of all mosquitoes - a full two inches from stem to stern. At that moment there is no doubt that if all mosquitoes were this size, the answer would be a definite yes!

Fortunately, what we have spotted is not a mosquito, but a cranefly. Crane flies, like hoverflies, are completely harmless insects. Although they look like large gangly mosquitoes, their mouths are adapted for sipping nectar, not blood.

There is no doubt that some insects can make our lives miserable. On the other hand, there is no sense in worrying about that which is harmless. So learn to distinguish the annoying insects from the impostors and you will find yourself enjoying the summer a whole lot more.

One interesting question I have about animals that mimic others is:

_____

_____

_____

_____

_____

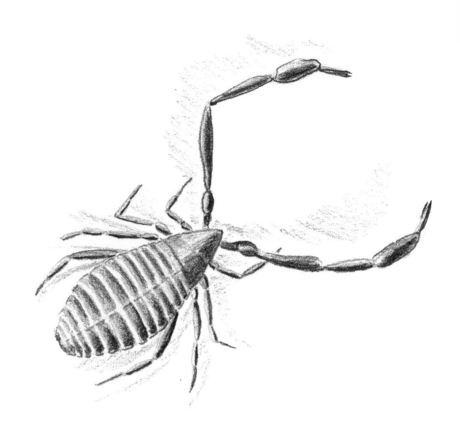

Some pseudoscorpions can be found in the home, often around old dusty books. They feed on booklice and mites and are called book scorpions.

4

Risks vs. Rewards

A **favorite activity:**
Find a quiet secluded spot in the woods where I will not be disturbed.

Plunk myself down on the ground, leaning against a tree for comfort.

Remain perfectly still, trying to become one with my surroundings.

Observe whatever wildlife comes my way.

Possible rewards:

Sighting of deer, squirrel, mink, woodpeckers, warblers, frogs, turtles, dragonflies, beetles, spiders, harvestmen, butterflies and countless other forms of wildlife.

Possible risks

Mosquitoes - mostly a minor annoyance.

Ticks - a tick check removes most of the danger.

All in all, the possible rewards far outweigh the possible dangers. In different parts of the country, the list of dangers could include bears, chiggers, poisonous snakes, brown recluse spiders and a whole host of other animals. A recent trip to the Florida Everglades reminded me of how benign our Northeast woods really are.

We had just paddled out to one of the islands in the Everglades National Park in southern Florida. While setting up our tents, Doug Lowry, one of our party, called us to come look at what he had found. Crawling on his tent was a three-inch scorpion. Being the nature lover he is, he picked up the scorpion - carefully - and tossed it into the brush behind his tent.

This simple action, probably a very common one in southern Florida and other parts of the country, sure did raise the excitement level of our camping trip. Now, something as mundane as putting on shoes in the morning became a small adventure. Had something sought refuge in there during the night - a bit of wildlife we were not too anxious to meet face to face?

After most of us had packed our gear and headed back home, Doug continued on his way island-hopping for another week. He met up with a couple that related this story: They had been partying it up one night (rather heavily it seems). The next morning, the woman awoke with a very sore shoulder. Looking at the digital photos they had taken during the party, they noticed in one of the pictures that she had a scorpion on her shoulder. Apparently, she had been stung the night before but hadn't noticed it at the time - thus, the conclusion the partying had been rather heavy.

While the sting of most scorpions is not life threatening, it is none-the-less rather painful and an experience everyone I know would prefer to avoid. And yet, the reward of seeing a scorpion was well worth the risk of being stung. But here in New England, seeing a scorpion is not an option. There are no scorpions in New England.

There are, however, pseudoscorpions but they do not pose much of a danger. Every time I sit myself down in the woods, I am probably sitting on hundreds of them. They are really quite small. In fact, they are so small - about 1/5th of an inch or smaller - that they are no threat whatsoever to humans. However, they sure are a terror to all the small creatures that live in the leaf litter on the forest floor, such as mites and springtails.

The easiest way to collect pseudoscorpions is to use a Berlese Funnel. The funnel holds the leaf litter. The heat from a light bulb above the funnel dries the leaf litter from the top down. As the leaf litter dries, the small creatures in the litter are forced to the bottom of the funnel, where they fall into a container. Of all the creatures I have collected this way, the pseudoscorpion is the most fearsome looking.

Pseudoscorpions, or "false scorpions", lack the stinger in the tail of real scorpions. But they do not lack weapons. The large claws in the front of most pseudoscorpions contain poison glands that are used to paralyze their prey. Once paralyzed, the pseudoscorpion bites its prey, injecting a saliva that dissolves the innards of its meal. It then slurps up its dinner.

The mouthparts of the pseudoscorpion also contain silk glands. The silk is used to make a cocoon where the pseudoscorpion will spend the winter. All in all, they might live 2 or 3 years.

To observe pseudoscorpions, you need a good magnifying glass or a dissecting microscope and a berlese funnel. You can find instructions to make a berlese funnel in the Nature Activities section of this book on page 75.

So this summer, take some time to sit in the woods and enjoy whatever nature brings your way. It is a perfectly safe way to pass a few enjoyable hours. And for a real reward, hunt up a few pseudoscorpions.

One interesting question I have about life in the leaf litter is:

_____

_____

_____

_____

Red maples grow in a wide variety of habitats, from dry sandy areas to swamps. Swamp red maples tend to produce less spectacular fall foliage than those growing on dry ground.

5

Mother Nature's Fashion Show

Old Mother Nature has really woven some magic
this year. The colors are stunning. Here come the oaks in a
lovely russet cloak. And look there, at the aspens, all decked
out in a splendid, golden-yellow number. But once again, the
crowd favorite has to be the red maples in their stunning scarlet
reds. Where do they come up with these color schemes?

If you are into fall foliage, New England is the place to be. Nowhere
else in the world can match the brilliance of our autumn display. And while
it is not possible to take the scenery for granted, it is possible to sometimes
get to thinking that the trees are decorating themselves solely for our
enjoyment. But nothing could be further from the truth. The leaf color is all
part of the survival scheme of the trees - some of this scheme is understood
by botanists, some still needs to be discovered.

Ask almost anyone what color leaves are and the answer you get is -
green. Except for a very short period just before leaves die, they are green.
Ask a botanist the same question and the answer you get is also green, as
well as some yellow and maybe orange. It's just that you can't see these
other colors until the green disappears in the fall, but they are there
nonetheless. *

The chemicals that give leaves their colors are called pigments. And
since trees are not interested in using their colors to attract a mate (like some

insects, birds and other animals), the pigments must have some other functions. Some of these functions are well understood by botanists, others have yet to give up their secrets.

Let's start off with the green color. This pigment is called *chlorophyll*. The job of the chlorophyll is to extract the energy from sunlight. This energy is used in the process of photosynthesis, the process by which plants make their food - sugar. In the summer, the leaves of trees are constantly making chlorophyll - and so the leaves look green.

However, in the autumn, as the days get shorter and the nights get cooler, a membrane, called the abscission layer, begins to grow between the leaf stem and the branch. This is where the leaf will eventually break off when it falls from the tree. This membrane also limits the flow of water and nutrients from the roots into the leaves, causing chlorophyll production to stop. Since chlorophyll breaks down rather quickly, it soon disappears from the leaf. The green color fades.

With the green gone, we can now see the yellows and oranges in the leaves, much like removing a forest green jacket to reveal a brightly colored Hawaiian shirt. These colors are due to a group of pigments called *carotenoids* . Since the carotenoids break down more slowly than the chlorophyll, their color remains in the leaf after the green chlorophyll has left. It is believed that the carotenoids assist the chlorophyll in photosynthesis, utilizing some of the sunlight not used by chlorophyll. Some trees contain more carotenoids than others. These trees, like the aspens, hickories and sugar maples turn bright yellow or orange in the fall.

Of course the colors that truly make the New England autumn spectacular are the reds, pinks and purples. These colors are due to the pigment *anthocyanin*. Anthocyanin is not found in the leaves during the summer, but is produced by some trees in the fall.

As mentioned earlier, sugars are produced in the leaves through photosynthesis. When the abscission layer forms at the base of the leaf stem, the sugars become trapped in the leaf. In some trees, this high sugar content triggers the production of anthocyanin, turning the leaf red. The shade of red (pink to purple) is determined by the acidity in the leaf.

It is not known what function the anthocyanin plays in the leaf, although some botanists think it may help protect the leaves from ultraviolet light - acting as a sort of plant suntan lotion.

Anyone who watches Mother Natures fashion show knows that some years are more spectacular than others. To predict a particularly good show, look for warm sunny days to promote photosynthesis and sugar production, and cool crisp nights causing the sugars to be trapped in the leaves to form the anthocyanins. Notice, however, that since the carotenoids are always present in the leaves, even a poor color year still yields the yellows and oranges. They just may not last very long.

* To reveal the hidden colors of the leaf, check out the Hidden Colors activity on page 79.

One interesting question I have about fall foliage is:

_____

_____

_____

_____

_____

Some beaches are literally
covered in Crepidula shells,
attesting to their large numbers
just offshore.

6

What If?

What if you moved into a new building complex; one that contained everything needed for life, one that you never needed to leave and couldn't if you wanted to.

What if you were the first person to move into the building? You were just waiting for others to move in - you were looking forward to companionship both of the same sex and the opposite sex.

What if the only people to move in were of the same sex? No one of the opposite sex would ever move into your building. If you wished to start a family - your greatest desire in life - you would have to take the initiative.

What if you were given one chance in your life to change your sex so you could start that family? Would you take that chance?

Crepidula , the slipper shell starts life as an egg. Tucked neatly away in a gelatinous egg mass by the mothers' foot, *Crepidula* takes about 2-4 weeks to develop into the larval, or young stage. Like most seashore life, the larval stage of *Crepidula* is spent wandering the oceans as part of the plankton. At this young stage, the veliger larva, as it is called, has a tiny shell and two wing-like structures with small hairs or cilia. These cilia enable the juvenile Crepidula to swim about, although in a very limited degree. They are also used to trap other, smaller plankton for food.

After leading this wandering life for about a month and a half, *Crepidula* is ready to settle down to a rather sedentary life.

The young *Crepidula* finally settles out of the plankton and hopefully lands on a hard substrate - either a rock or stack of other *Crepidula* shells. At this stage of life, all young *Crepidula* are males. For a short while, they are capable of slowly crawling around looking for a suitable home. As they grow, their shell grows to fit their surroundings. By the time they are two years old, they are home for life - incapable of further movement.

Once firmly established on its home, *Crepidula* is very hard to dislodge. It is completely sealed to its substrate with the exception of two openings at its front end. One opening lets water in. The plankton contained in the water is filtered out by *Crepidula's* gills. This plankton is compressed into a pellet, which is directed to the mouth. *Crepidulas'* tongue carries the food into the mouth. The water exits through the second opening.

If a young male *Crepidula* lands on a bare rock, it quickly looses its male reproductive organs and develops into a female. If, however, it lands on a female *Crepidula*, it remains a male as long as the female underneath it remains alive. Should other young male *Crepidulas* land on this male, he may develop female reproductive organs and for a while exist as both male and female at the same time. If the bottom female should die, he/she is ready to loose the male reproductive organs and live the rest of her 5-10 years as a female. Once a female, she can never go back to being a male.

In a large stack of *Crepidula*, the bottom one is always a female, the top ones are males and the in-between ones are both at the same time.

Unlike our hypothetical question at the beginning of the story, the *Crepidula* has no say in the matter. It can't decide for itself which sex to be. All *Crepidula* start life as males and will remain so if they are attached to a female. If the female dies, the male at the bottom of the pile develops into a female. This seems to be regulated by pheromones or chemicals given off by the living female. As long as these female chemicals are produced, males can't become fully female. When these chemicals disappear and a female is needed for the community, a new one is formed.

What if you had one chance in life to change sex so you could start a family? What if, like *Crepidula*, you had no say in the matter?

One interesting question I have about
sea creatures is:

_____

_____

_____

_____

_____

_____

Caught in the glow of a porch light, winter moths remind one of a snowstorm.

7

Winter Moths

Another New England winter is approaching. Most people I know dread the approach of winter as much as they do the winter itself. The thought of being cold for the next six months is enough to put anyone in a bad mood. But, as bad as winter is for us, it is even tougher on our insects. That is because with the first good frost, most insects die. There are, however, a number of insects that don't perish with the cold. Many of these survive by burrowing under ground below the frost line while others fill their bodies with anti-freeze compounds that allow them to pass the winter in a deep sleep, only waking up with the warmer weather of the spring.

This absence of insects helps dictate the community of animals found in our New England landscape. Insect-eating birds like warblers and vireos must migrate to warmer, insect-bearing climates if they are to find food. Our native bats would also starve in the winter. Some of them follow the birds south while others hibernate until their food reappears in the spring.

With the predators gone, it is not surprising that a few insects have adapted to the cold and carry out their business in the relative safety of the predator-free winter. Of these insects, the easiest to spot are the moths. Our winter moths are usually a mottled brown color and about 1 inch in length. To find them, all you need to do is turn on your porch light during a winter thaw. You may be rewarded with dozens of these creatures attracted to the lights. What you are seeing are the male winter moths. Only the males. The females are wingless and cannot fly.

How is it that these delicate creatures can survive the winter while most insects can't? At first it was thought that perhaps these moths had anti-freeze in their blood like some of the hibernating insects. But this turned out not to be the case. In fact, it was discovered that if their body temperature dropped much below freezing, they would die just as surely as most of our other insects. Therefore, they must have some unusual ways of keeping their bodies warm.

During the cold winters days and nights, these moths spend their time sleeping beneath the leaf litter in the forest. Scientists measuring the temperature beneath the leaves have discovered that it rarely drops below 35 degrees even when the air temperature drops well below that (see Life in the Leaf Litter Activity, page 93). The moths stay put during these cold spells. It is only during the warmer winter thaws that the moths can emerge and fly around. But to fly, the moth's body temperature must be around 85 degrees! How can the moth warm its body to 85 degrees in the winter?

Shivering! The only way to generate that kind of heat in the winter is by shivering. We do the same thing. When we are cold, we shiver. This is the body's method of producing extra heat. To warm up it's body to flight temperature, the moth shivers. Once the body is warm, it must stay warm. Unlike our summer moths, the winter moth's body is covered with a special "fur". This fur lining helps the moth retain the heat it has generated.

Getting warm and flying around in a predator-free environment is all well and good. But getting warm and flying requires a lot of energy. Most moths feed on nectar from flowers. However, there are no flowers blooming in the winter. So these moths must tap another food source - tree sap, the same stuff from which maple syrup is made.

Finding the male winter moth is easy. Just turn on an outside light and you will see plenty. They congregate in large numbers around lights. Finding the females, however, is a little more difficult. Since they are wingless, they cannot fly to the light. Instead, look for them on the trunk of trees. A little patience is needed for they are well camouflaged. However, a good flashlight and a magnifying glass will make the task a

winter moth male and female

little easier. Once you find one and know what to look for, you will begin to discover lots of them. Looking closely at the female, you might notice she is not covered with fur like the male. So, how does she stay warm in the winter?

One interesting question I have about winter animals is:

_____

_____

_____

_____

_____

_____

In any pond or slow stream, a dip net
scraped along the bottom will bring
up many decaying leaves. This is a
great place to look for aquatic
animals.

8

A Life of Community Service

One day this past autumn, I was standing by a stream watching the falling leaves. One leaf landed in the stream in front of me and was immediately carried away by the current and disappeared from view. It passed without a sound, and had I not been standing at the stream at that exact time, its passing would have occurred totally unnoticed. After all, it was just one of perhaps 200,000 leaves on a tree, which was just one tree of the thousands that line the stream where they have been shedding their leaves for millions of years. Such a small insignificant event, yet it got me thinking. If this leaf had never existed, would it have made any difference in the world? Would its absence have been noticed? Where did it come from? Where will it end? And what good did it do along the way?

Leaves are literally made from air and water. Trees take up carbon dioxide from the air–0.03% of air is carbon dioxide- and water from the ground. Using the energy from sunlight, these two molecules are broken down during photosynthesis, and recombined as the sugar glucose. Some of this sugar is used to produce cellulose, the stuff that makes up leaves, and the rest of the tree.

During its life on the tree, the leaf is busy taking in carbon dioxide and water, and converting them into more sugar. This sugar is not only the raw material for cellulose; it is also the food – the energy source – of the tree. In a process called respiration, the sugar is split back into its component parts of carbon dioxide and water, releasing the energy originally stored in the sugar, making it available to be used in all the biological processes of the tree.

In this way, the leaf, along with all of its sister leaves, provides all the food required by the tree.

Feeding a tree may seem like a pretty big job, but the leaf does not stop there. Any number of animals – from insects to deer –also use the sugar produced by the leaf as food. You only need to look at the leaves of a tree to see where others have chewed through the leaf, sucked out its contents, scraped its surface, tunneled through its interior or in some other way benefited from the bounty of the leaf. At any one time, the leaves of a tree may be feeding thousands of other creatures.

The leaf's service to others doesn't end with its death. When the leaf drops into the river in the fall, it is immediately attacked by fungi. The fungi begin to break down the leaf, utilizing the sugar stored within as its food source. During this time of decay, a whole succession of different fungi will feed on the leaf, each in its own turn.

Once the leaf has reached a sufficient level of decay, it is ready to be of service to another group of living organisms – the leaf shredders. The leaf, or bits of the leaf, now traveling along the bottom of the stream, will feed a whole host of aquatic insect larvae such as caddisflies, stoneflies and craneflies. They will chew up the leaf into finer and finer particles, extracting the nutrients as they go.

To finish off any nutrients left in the original leaf, the bacteria will now take their turn.

Even though the leaf is now completely decomposed, its service to others is not yet done. Waste products from all those that fed on the leaf – products that originated in the leaf - are carried downstream to nourish many of the single celled organisms that make up the plankton, single celled plants and animals that float with the current. Also benefiting from the leaf are the grazers and predators that feed on the fungi, insects and bacteria that initially took their nourishment from the leaf. Even though these grazers and predators do not feed directly from the leaf, it is still the leaf's nutrients that eventually find their way to these animals.

The falling leaves are not a part of the stream habitat per se, however their importance to all the creatures in the stream cannot be understated. It is their service of providing a food source long after the leaf has died that sustains the life in our streams. Such a small insignificant event like a leaf falling in a stream is a matter of life and death to so many.

One interesting question I have about trees is:

_____

_____

_____

_____

_____

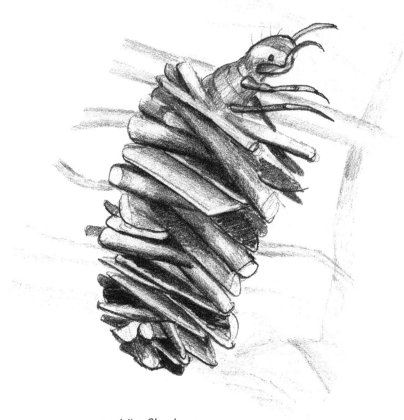

caddisfly larva

Different species of caddisflies make their home from different materials - they may use twigs, pebbles, sand, bark, grass etc.

9

Through the Looking Glass

The thought of creatures as strange as a caddisfly larvae had intrigued a friend of mine ever since she read about them in an article I had written for an environmental newsletter. Since then, she had peered into the river in search of one every time she went kayaking. At work, the next day, she would report, "No caddisfly larvae." Again and again, I would hear the same refrain, "No caddisfly larvae." I could see that she was beginning to despair of ever seeing one of these fascinating creatures. Did they really exist or had I just made them up?

One day at the end of January a few years back, she came to work, grinning from ear to ear. "Guess what I saw?" she asked. Instantly I knew what had happened. Against all odds, conditions had been just perfect the night before. The water and the air temperature were just right. There was absolutely no wind at all. It was the end of January and there was no snow. The water had frozen so completely, so fast that the ice was as clear as glass. The next day was a bright sunny day, with the sunlight shining down through the ice and lighting up the world below.

Lucy and her family, out for a walk, were crossing the ice when she knelt down to peer below. Because of the conditions, she could see clearly everything happening under the ice. And the world revealed below her looking glass of ice was in many ways just as strange as the world Alice found through her looking glass!

"Come quick," she called to her family. "There is a stick under the ice that has sprouted legs and is walking away!" At that instant, she knew she had seen her first caddisfly larva. At that instant, the grin spread across her face and stayed there until she came into my office the next day.

Soon, the whole family was belly down on the ice peering below. There were multicolored little beetles swimming around, each with a silvery edge about their folded wings. Adult insects must breath air like us. And just like us, if they wish to stay submerged for extended periods, they must bring their air supply with them. To do this, they trap an air bubble under their wings. In this position, the air bubble is in contact with their spiracles, tiny breathing holes along the sides of their bellies. Scuba-diving beetles!

Looking closely in the muck, they could see the outline of a dragonfly larva, almost completely buried. Perfectly still, yet completely aware and awake, it was waiting for a smaller insect to forget it was there and swim a little too near. Faster than the eye could follow, it would dart forward, and with its lower lip, snare the insect, eat it and settle down for another wait.

One curious insect was hanging upside down from a submerged plant. Letting go of the plant, it began beating its legs back and forth, swimming very rapidly in jerky little motions upside down, almost as if it were peering back out through the ice at my friends. It spends its whole adult life upside down. Appropriately called a "Backswimmer", it is a type of bug, with a sharp, beak-like mouth that it inserts into smaller insects to suck out their juices.

Other bugs were to be seen also. Lumbering through the algae was a Giant Water Bug, about two inches long, oval in shape and dark, dark brown in color. This fearsome looking beast can give a nasty bite. One of its nicknames is "Toe Biter". However nasty these bugs may seem, they are the truly politically correct bugs of the aquatic world, for it is the male that cares for the young. The eggs are glued onto his back where he will care for them until they hatch.

Of all the strange and wonderful sights my friend and her family saw that day, the strangest was sighted by her son. "Wow, you gotta see this thing," he shouted. There, crawling upside-down along the under surface of the ice was a gigantic Dobsonfly larva. Three inches long with a pair of filaments stretching out from each body segment, it looked like a giant underwater centipede. The dobsonfly larva, or hellgrammite, is the undisputed king of this underwater world, using its strong jaws to catch anything within reach, including small fish.

This was a very special day for my friend and her family. Only under these ideal conditions can one get such a clear view of this magical underwater world. Only in the dead of winter, when the land seems so lifeless, does the river truly reveal its life.

CAUTION: Before venturing out on the ice, you should make sure it is safe to walk on. Generally, it should be 4 inches thick to insure safety. After all, you only want to observe the life in the pond, not join it.

One interesting question I have about creatures that live in the river is:

_____

_____

_____

_____

_____

Winter fireflies often use the
same tree year after year. Look
for them on a thick-barked tree
with a good southern exposure.

10

Chasing Fireflies

I went chasing fireflies today.

Those five words are usually enough to evoke childhood memories of warm, summer, nights, running through the fields with a net and a mason jar full of glowing fireflies. So you might be surprised to learn that the "today" I am speaking of is not in the summer, and it is not at night, and my fireflies aren't glowing.

"Today" is February 11. While it is rather warm for February here in New England – about 60 degrees – there is still a foot of snow on the ground. The time is 2:00 in the afternoon. My fireflies are not glowing because they can't. They don't have light organs.

Ellychnia corrusca is one of the many types of fireflies that live here in Massachusetts. *Ellychnia corrusca* is the scientific name. They have no common name, so I will just refer to them as *Ellychnia*. While they look like just about any other kind of firefly, they have evolved a very different lifestyle than the fireflies with which we are so familiar.

We think of fireflies as creatures of the summer. The adults live for only a few weeks during the warm weather – just long enough to attract a mate and lay their eggs. Then they die. The larval fireflies spend the winter under ground, usually for a couple of years, and then they emerge in late spring or summer as adults.

Ellychnia is on a different time schedule. The adults first appear in late August, after other fireflies are gone. They feed on the nectar of fall plants until the approach of winter. Then they find an appropriate place to ride out the winter. One good choice for them is a crevice in the bark of a thick-barked tree like the white oak. Here, they somehow survive the cold and wait for the coming of spring. When the weather begins to warm, usually in March, but occasionally on a warm day in February, they become active again. This is the time to go firefly chasing. They are pretty easy to spot, walking along the bark of the trees looking for a mate, or having found one, attached to their mate end to end. They may search for a mate on the tree where they spent the winter, or they may leave the tree and look elsewhere. In past years, I have often seen fireflies fly around and alight on the side of my house in early spring. At the time, I didn't know what I was looking at and was surprised to see fireflies so early in the year, and equally surprised to see them active during the day. Now I know.

Daytime fireflies have no need to flash. The flashes would not show up on a bright sunny day. Therefore, they don't have light organs and couldn't flash if they wanted to. If you catch a firefly and turn it over to look at its abdomen, you will see that either the second to last segment or the last two segments are white, depending on the type of firefly and its sex. These are the light organs. If, however, you don't see these white segments on the abdomen, you are looking at one of the daytime fireflies like *Ellychnia*.

Most fireflies use their flash to attract a mate. Since *Ellychnia* can't flash, it must have some other method of attracting a mate. It does this with chemical signals called pheromones. This is not nearly as spectacular to those of us who watch fireflies, but it works for them just the same.

Scientists believe that in the not too distant past, *Ellychnia*'s ancestors were active during the summer, flew at night and had the ability to glow, just like most fireflies. However, something caused them to slowly evolve the habits they exhibit today. The scientists speculate that the something was... other fireflies.

If you catch a firefly and give it a little pinch, you might notice that you caused it to bleed. As long as you haven't pinched too hard and actually injured it, this bleeding was done on purpose. It is called *reflexive bleeding*. These fireflies are exuding blood from around their leg joints and wings. This blood contains a poisonous chemical that will deter other animals from trying to eat them. The chemical is potent enough to kill lizards many times the size of the firefly, as some people have found out with dismay, when they tried to feed fireflies to their pet lizards.

Most of our native fireflies have this poison in their blood. However, there is one group of fireflies, *Photuris,* that can't make the poison. The only way they can acquire it is to eat other fireflies and assimilate the poison for their own use. These *Photuris* fireflies have learned to imitate the flash signal of the females of other types of firefly, luring the hapless males to their doom. This predation of one firefly by another causes the flashing signals of fireflies to evolve rather rapidly – a firefly with a flash that is not known to *Photuris* has a better chance of survival therefore enabling it to mate and pass on this new flash pattern to its offspring. Until, that is, the *Photuris* fireflies have had time to learn that pattern and the whole process starts again.

Ellychnia avoids this predation issue by being active during the day when it is possible to see who is trying to attract you, and by conducting your business before the *Photuris* fireflies have arrived on the scene.

All of which means we humans can enjoy chasing fireflies of one type or another spring, summer and fall, and, if we are lucky, even on a balmy winter day.

Many scientists believe that firefly populations are disappearing. You may have noticed far fewer fireflies as an adult than you did as a kid. But, to really understand what is happening to fireflies, scientists need a lot of actual data, to do a firefly census. If you would like to help the scientists collect this data, and learn more about fireflies in the process, consider joining the Firefly Watch Citizen Science program at the Museum of Science. You can check it out at www.mos.org/fireflywatch.

One interesting question I have about nighttime creatures is:

_____

_____

_____

_____

If you see a school of whirligigs
sitting quietly in the water, toss a
small twig among them. Do they
investigate it, start whirling, or dive
for the bottom?

11

Whirligig Beetles

When asked what his study of nature had taught him about religion, a famous scientist said that God must be inordinately fond of beetles. That was because of all species of living creatures, the majority are by far the insects. And of all species of insects, the majority are by far the beetles.

Beetles can be divided into two groups; those that live in the water and those that live out of it. Doubtless, you are familiar with the beetles that live out of the water, the terrestrial insects. If you have never seen the beetles that live in the water, that is soon remedied. Just peer into any pond or slow-moving river and you will see them walking on the bottom or swimming from hiding place to hiding place, carrying a bubble of air under their wings for breathing. The whirligig beetle can't seem to decide which of the two groups it belongs to. So it compromises; half of its body is in the water and half is out. It lives at the water's surface. It is a creature of two worlds. This dual existence doubles its opportunities as well as its dangers.

Death can strike the whirligig from above the water's surface, at the surface or from below it. If the threat is from above or below, the whirligig uses its eyes to detect it. Like most insects, the whirligig beetle has a pair of compound eyes. The whirligig's eyes, however, are divided into two halves, one half on the top of the head looking up, the other half on the bottom of the head looking down! This allows the whirligig to notice both aerial and aquatic predators.

If the threat approaches from the surface, the whirligig relies on its antennae. The antennae are held out in front of the beetle along the water's surface. The waves created by an approaching animal will move the antenna up and down, alerting the whirligig of its approach.

Whirligigs can be seen at the surface in large groups called schools. They are shiny black beetles, oval in shape and a quarter to a half inch in length. The second and third pair of legs are short and flat, like oars. These are the legs used for swimming. Each paddle-like leg will propel them forward about a half inch, producing no surface ripple. When threatened, however, they move quite rapidly, swimming in tight spirals. This motion gives them the name "Whirligig". The whole school is one tight spiraling mass of beetles, seemingly gone mad. Try watching one beetle, as if you were a predator and wanted that particular one for dinner. It is easy to see how the predator would become confused.

But for all the confusion, the beetles seem to know exactly what they are doing. If you watch closely, you will notice the beetles never bump into each other. As the beetles move, they create ripples. It may be these ripples that tell them when they are too close to each other and must turn to avoid a collision.

When disturbed, the whirligigs may also dive under the water and head for cover. Often they will secrete a substance that is bad-tasting. One type of whirligig gives off an odor of ripe apples, others just smell vile. Try catching a whirligig and see what it smells like.

As I write this article in early February, the adult whirligigs are fast asleep, hibernating in the mud at the bottom of the ponds and streams. They will emerge in the early spring, mate, lay their eggs on underwater plants, then die. They won't reappear until, after a few months, the eggs have hatched and the larvae have grown to adults. Then in late summer, they will be back on the surface until winter brings hibernating time.

Those of us who spend a lot of time in the outdoors are always on the lookout for signs of spring, such as the red-winged blackbird or spring peepers. Perhaps the whirligig would be a more useful indicator. It's appearance would not only announce the coming of spring, but also the ending of summer!

One interesting question I have about pond creatures is:

_____

_____

_____

_____

_____

_____

Any damage to the bark of a tree,
whether made by an insect, bird
or human, may be the beginning of
the end for the tree.

12

Dead or Alive

In the woods near my house stood a most majestic tree. This tree, an Eastern Hemlock, with a trunk a full two feet in diameter, was the prince of my forest. It was a tree I admired for its beauty as well as its strength. That is, until it died one night in a windstorm. It just snapped in two about 10 feet from the ground.

I mourned for that tree. It provided shade and shelter for the creatures in and around it. It was food for the deer, roosting and nesting sites for the birds, and home and hearth to countless numbers of insects. Its passing would leave a void in the forest – an emptiness I would notice every time I walked past its rotting carcass. As near as I can tell, this is what happened to my tree. Where the tree had snapped, I noticed a few tunnels bored through the middle of the tree – each about the diameter of a finger. The wood around these tunnels was rather soft and spongy. I am guessing that the tunnels were the work of the larva of a long-horned wood-boring beetle. And the sponginess was from that of a fungus.

As a group, the long-horned wood-borers are some of our most colorful and largest beetles. I have seen a three-inch beetle land on a tree followed closely by a woodpecker. The woodpecker considered it for a while, figuring it for a meal since it was an insect and that is what woodpeckers eat. But the beetle was fully half the size of the bird. Eventually, the woodpecker took off, searching for easier prey.

The wood-borers lay their eggs on the bark of a tree. When the eggs hatch, they will eat their way through the bark and into the wood. They continue eating their way through the wood, their tunnels getting larger as they grow. As full-grown larva, they will pupate, turn into adults and exit the tree. It was the tunnels of the larva that I saw in the hemlock stump.

There are many fungi that attack trees. But for all the damage they can do, they can't get past the tree bark. They must wait for a door to open for them to get inside and do their mischief. Once the wood-borer larvae chew their way through the bark, the door is open for the fungus. The spores of the fungus might be blown in by the wind, washed in with the rain or carried in on the insect itself. However it happens, the fungus is in. When the spores germinate, they send out thin threads called hyphae. These hyphae give off chemicals that break down the cells of the wood. The hyphae feed off the nutrients released from the broken cells. As the wood cells break down, the hyphae extend further through the tree, feeding as they go. The destroyed wood becomes spongy, looses its strength, and the tree snaps in two in a high wind. This is what I think killed my tree.

There are a number of beetles that can burrow through the bark of a tree. Whether it be a long-horned wood-borer, a powder post beetle, or bark engraver, the process has begun. These insects do relatively little damage to the tree. But they lead the way for the real killers – the fungi. Once the fungi get in, they can send their hyphae throughout the tree, weakening the wood until the tree breaks. The only sign that fungi are at work is when they grow their reproductive structures. Think of the hard shelf-like mushrooms growing on the side of a tree. These reproductive structures are commonly called "conks". By the time you see these on a tree, the end is inevitable.

Once the tree falls, there is a rather orderly progression of events that occurs. Bacteria and other fungi will enter through the wounds, continuing the process of decomposition. A number of predacious beetles enter the tunnels to feed on the wood-boring beetles. Small arthropods such as springtails move in to feed on the bacteria and fungus. Predatory mites soon follow, feeding on the springtails. As the fungi and bacteria break down the tree further, the rotting wood becomes ideal germinating medium for seeds of other forest plants. The roots of these plants spread throughout the tree, continuing the process of decomposition. The spongy, rotting wood soaks up and holds moisture making it a haven during a dry spell. Moisture and insects are everything a salamander could ask for. Soon there are tunnels throughout the wood that are large enough for small mammals such as voles.

This process goes on for twenty to many hundreds of years, depending on the tree species and environmental conditions. During that time, thousands of plants and animals will call the tree home. There is truly no greater place to look for life in the forest than a dead tree. Rather than leaving a void by dying, my hemlock has created a living community that I shall enjoy for many years to come.

One interesting question I have about a fungus is:

_____

_____

_____

_____

_____

_____

Although bumble bees usually nest underground, I once found one in the attic of my house.

13

The Bumblebee

Ah, summer at last! Of all the treats that summer brings, I especially like its sounds. Nothing conjures up visions of the glorious summer days ahead like the late afternoon song of the robin, the lazy drone of the bumblebee or the wind rustling through the leaves of an aspen tree. But wait! That bumblebee sounds upset, desperate or frantic – anything but lazy. Let's investigate.

Following the loud buzzing sound to its source is easy. There she is in plain sight, stuck in the middle of that flower. Is she in the grip of some venomous arachnid - a camouflaged spider we can't see? Or, is this some new type of carnivorous plant that lured the bumblebee to a hideous death by slowly being dissolved by powerful digestive juices? No, it's nothing quite so melodramatic. She is actually very peacefully going about her business collecting pollen to bring back to the hive to feed her queen and sisters.

Look closely. Even though the bumblebee is making a loud buzzing sound, her wings aren't moving. She has disconnected her wings from the muscles that move them. The muscles (but not the wings) are vibrating rapidly, causing her whole body to vibrate rapidly. This, in turn, causes the flower she is sitting on to vibrate rapidly. The pollen is shaken loose from the anthers on which it grows and goes flying in all directions, much of it falling onto the bumblebee. She then brushes the pollen off her body and deposits it onto the two pollen baskets on her hind legs. A bee that has been foraging for some time will have two large yellow or orange pollen balls stuck to her pollen baskets, the color determined by the type of flowers she has been visiting.

This type of pollination, called "buzz pollination", makes bumblebees very efficient pollinators of certain types of flowers. These flowers, such as blueberries and tomatoes, have hollow anthers with a hole at the end. The pollen, which forms inside the anthers, is shaken out of the anthers by the rapid vibrations of the bumblebee. For this reason, it is bumblebees, and not honeybees (which do not buzz pollinate), that are used in greenhouses to pollinate tomatoes.

Now that you know that the bumblebee is not upset, get a little closer, and take a good look. Notice the lovely coat she is wearing – a covering of thick black and yellow hair. Many insects have a coating of hair, but none have the beautiful thick pile of our bumblebee. This must be a very warm coat indeed!

By vibrating the flight muscles, the bumblebee can generate considerable heat. This process is called shivering, something we humans also do when we need to warm our bodies.

Because of this shivering ability to warm itself, and because of the thick hair and large body size, which aids in insulation, the bumblebee is able to visit flowers at much colder temperatures than its cousin the honeybee. Try keeping a record of which bee is the first to visit the flowers in the spring and the last in the fall. It will come as no surprise that the bumblebee will win every time.

Since the bumblebee has this ability to raise her temperature, she will do something that her smaller cousin can't do. Like a mother bird, the queen bumblebee will sit on her eggs to incubate them.

A bumblebee nest is a one year affair. Only the new queens survive the winter. All others; workers, drones (the males) and old queens succumb to the cold. Since they are starting from scratch and alone, the queens must start early, even though the ground is still cold. The most likely place for the bumblebee nest is underground, in an old mouse or chipmunk nest.

On the floor of the nest, the young queen will construct a tiny cup of wax and fill it with nectar. This "honeypot" will serve as an emergency supply of food for days when the weather is too harsh for the queen to venture forth. Next, she will fashion a small wax covered ball of pollen in which she will lay about 4 to 20 eggs. To help the eggs hatch more quickly, she will lie on the egg ball and shiver, raising her temperature and thereby the temperature of her eggs. The sooner her first batch of young are grown, the sooner they can take over most of the chores and she can concentrate on egg laying.

If you are feeling comfortable with the bumblebee now, you might get a little closer still. Do you see the balls of pollen stuck to the pollen baskets on her hind legs? If not, take a real close look at the legs again. Some types of bumblebees do not have the pollen baskets on their hind legs because they do not collect pollen. These bumblebees, called "cuckoo bumblebees", are freeloaders – or parasites in scientific terms.

The cuckoo bumblebees emerge later from hibernation than regular bumblebees. They have no need to get an early start to their season. Biding their time until the regular bumblebees nests are well under way, the cuckoo bumblebee will invade a nest and lay her eggs alongside those of the bumblebee. When the eggs hatch, the bumblebees will care for them as if they are their own sisters. It has been noticed that once the cuckoo bumblebees eggs have hatched, no more bumblebee young are produced. It is not certain why this is, but with no new bumblebees being produced, the nest soon declines.

Since the cuckoo bumblebees do no work, they do not need any workers. There are no worker cuckoo bumblebees, only drones and queens. The drones fertilize the queens and the queens parasitize the bumblebees.

As you are looking for the pollen baskets on the bumblebee, you do not want to get too close. While bumblebees are usually gentle and slow to ire, they can sting if provoked. And sting again. And again! Honeybee's stingers are barbed and remain in your skin. When the honeybee flies away, the stinger and part of her body remain behind, killing the honeybee. Bumblebee stingers are not barbed so they can jab and jab again, then fly away intact.

A loud buzzing from the bumblebee on a flower indicates a busy, contented bumblebee. I do not know the sound an angry bumblebee makes. I have never made one angry. Nor do I wish to.

One interesting question I have about bumblebees is:

_____

_____

_____

_____

_____

This space reserved for
Nature Drawings
from my backyard

Try tickling a spider web with a
piece of grass. Can you convince
the spider that you are an insect
caught in the web?

14

The Perfect Predator

What image does these words bring to mind? To some, it is a pride of lions hunting the plains of the Serengeti; others might think of a shark prowling the coastal waters; or a crocodile lying in wait at the rivers edge.

In fact, the perfect predator lives right here in my backyard. It is the spider; or rather, spiders as a group. There is no place more dangerous for a small prey animal than my back yard. Death lurks in every bush and bramble, every crack and crevice, every blade of grass. Death can strike from any direction, any time of night or day. Death is the concern of every small creature that inhabits my back yard, a death that I am totally unaware of unless I make a special effort to seek it out.

One summer night I went looking for Death. With flashlight and magnifying glass in hand, I went hunting for the perfect predator.

It took a few minutes for my sensory awareness to diminish to the scale necessary, but before long, I started to see the predators. Two days earlier, I had seen a large moth wrapped in silk, attached to a bush, so I knew where to begin my search. In the glare of the flashlight, I found a large orb weaving spider perched in the center of a 15 inch web. The moth was now gone, sucked dry and discarded. In its place was an assassin bug, as large as the spider and just as deadly. Its days of terrorizing the neighborhood were clearly over. It too was shrouded in silk, waiting for the spider to regain her appetite.

Orb webs are the most easily recognized webs. These webs contain many straight lines of silk, radiating out from the central hub. Overlaying these straight threads is a line of sticky thread, spiraling outwards from the center. It is this sticky, spiral thread that captures the prey. Some of the webs can get to be two to three feet in diameter with the spiders  reaching about two inches from leg tip to leg tip. Most orb webs are much smaller with the web spanning a distance of two inches and the spider being not much larger than the period at the end of this sentence. Either way, both webs spell death for some unfortunate small creature. Every good-sized tree might easily contain a few of the larger spiders and thousands of the small ones.

Not all orb webs contain sticky threads. One group of orb weavers uses a very very fine thread, so fine that an insect will easily become entangled in it. These webs can be identified by the slightly bluish color of the silk.

The insects living in my back yard must worry about more than just orb webs. Sheet webs are just as dangerous. The sheet web consists of a single layer of non-sticky silk with a jumble of aerial lines above it. Any insect flying into the aerial lines falls onto the sheet. The spider, waiting under the sheet, bites the insect through the sheet and pulls it below where it can feed in relative safety.

Many of these sheetwebs can be found at the base of trees or under rocks or fallen logs. In some instances, the sheets are no longer flat, but stretched into a curved shape. The Dome Spider and the Bowl and Doily Spider are two very common spiders that spin their webs on low bushes and tall grass. The name of the spider is very suggestive of the shape of the web. An early

 morning walk, with the dew to highlight them, will reveal a web every foot or two across a large field.

Insects attempting to travel under these webs may find another challenge - funnel web spiders. These spiders build their webs in the grass. The webs are flat sheets of non-sticky silk with a tube or funnel at one corner of the web

leading to a hiding place. When an insect steps onto the web, the spider races across the web, bites the insect and drags it back into the funnel to eat it.

While many spider webs are beautifully designed, the cobweb spiders seem to have no discernible pattern to their webs. But many insects soon learn that they are just as efficient and deadly as any other web. Look for cobwebs in rock walls, brush piles or under the eaves of buildings. If you find one, chances are you will find a wrapped insect in the web as well as the spider.

If an insect manages to evade all webs (it is a tribute to the sheer numbers of insects that many do) it must still run a gauntlet of spiders. Coursing over the leaves of the trees and bushes are the jumping spiders, ready to pounce on anything that moves. Down below, patrolling the ground between the funnel webs are the wolf spiders. Both of these spiders actively chase down their prey. With their large eyes, they can often be spotted in the beam of a flashlight. The eyes glow like a cat caught in a set of headlights.

Other spiders are content to wait for the prey to come to them. A close inspection of flowers will reveal the crab spiders. Mostly daytime feeders, these spiders will sit motionless in the flower until some unsuspecting honeybee or other nectar feeder should wander too close. Often, a bee sitting unnaturally still in a flower indicates the presence of a crab spider.

Still other spiders might jump out of a hole in the ground, or dive through the surface of the water, or even throw their web at a passing insect. You might even find the spider that catches its prey by spitting at it.

Spiders have left no stone unturned in their search for food. They are the perfect predator. Which must mean that insects are the perfect prey. And I am content to be the perfect observer.

One interesting question I have about spiders is:

_____

_____

_____

_____

_____

This space reserved for

Nature Drawings

from my backyard

In one walk
through my back
yard, I captured over 30 deer
flies!

15

Dive Bombers

The Isles of Shoals in the springtime is a magical place. This group of nine islands six miles off the coast of Portsmouth, NH is a birder's paradise, a stopping place for birds migrating across the open ocean. Appledore Island, the largest of the islands is also the site of a college campus. A visit to the campus in the spring presents one with a rather strange sight. Outside every door of every building is a pile of sticks.

Appledore Island is, before all else, a gull nesting island. Both black-back and herring gulls nest on this tiny island by the thousands. In fact, during the height of breeding season, one would be hard pressed to walk 20 feet without stepping on a gull egg or chick. Obviously the parent gulls are none too thrilled with this situation and they do what many other parent animals do - they attack. Dive bomb would be a more precise term. They aim at the highest point of the intruder, the head. A peck on the head from a sharp gull's beak is sufficient to give one a nasty gash.

To walk anywhere on Appledore Island is to be attacked by gulls. So whenever possible, it is wise to walk next to a much taller person. When this is not possible, a gull stick is the next best remedy. Since the gulls attack the highest object, a stick held above the head attracts the gull's ire along with their beak. Whenever leaving a building for a walk across the island, it is wise to grab a stick from the pile outside each door and give the gulls a target higher than your head.

My back yard in the summer is a magical place. This three acre plot of land in Pembroke is a naturalist's delight that includes a field, hemlock forest, swamp and river. And like Appledore Island, my back yard is also the home of a dive bomber. This dive bomber is much smaller than a gull, but just as likely to draw blood, and all for the benefit of its offspring. I am referring to the female deer fly.

Like the mosquito, the female deer fly needs a blood meal to help her eggs develop. And like the mosquito, it is only the females that bite. However, where the mosquito will insert a needlelike mouth and suck blood, the deer fly cuts open the skin and laps up the blood. This hurts!

Deer flies are ambush predators. They sit in the vegetation and wait until they see moving prey. Then, like the gulls, they will attack the highest point of their prey - the head. For some reason, they like to circle the head and buzz it for a while before landing for a meal. Sometimes, they will start their attack at the edge of the woods and continue their head buzzing as I cross the field until they find a suitable place to bite or until I reach the house and I escape unscathed. As can be imagined, a healthy crop of hungry, dive-bombing deer flies following you around the back yard can quickly turn paradise into purgatory.

In the past, I have had two techniques for dealing with deer flies, neither one very satisfactory. The first is to swat at the flies and to slap at my head where I think they have landed. And since I am paranoid about getting bitten, I am always slapping my head. This technique is not very effective although very entertaining for my neighbors (watching safely from a screened porch).

The second is to wear a lot of clothes, including a hat. Offering as little naked skin as possible reduces the possible feeding surfaces for the fly, and the hat makes the head buzzing less annoying. This second technique is more effective than the first, but not very comfortable on a hot summer day.

A while ago, I learned a third technique for dealing with these pesky flies. In this technique, it is the dive-bombing habit of the deer fly that will be its undoing. It employs a "deer fly" stick. To make one, place a large plastic cup (research shows that blue is the optimal color) upside-down on the stick. Cover the cup with Tanglefoot, a very sticky material. Any deer fly buzzing the cup will stick - forever.

A trip to my neighborhood this summer should present one with a rather strange sight. Outside every door of every building, expect to see a pile of sticks with blue cups attached. And many deer flies attached to the cup. And you can find me, once again, able to enjoy the delights of my back yard.

For more information on the deer fly trap, check out the web site:

http://ufinsect.ifas.ufl.edu/deerfly_trap.htm

One interesting question I have about
flies is:

_____

_____

_____

_____

_____

_____

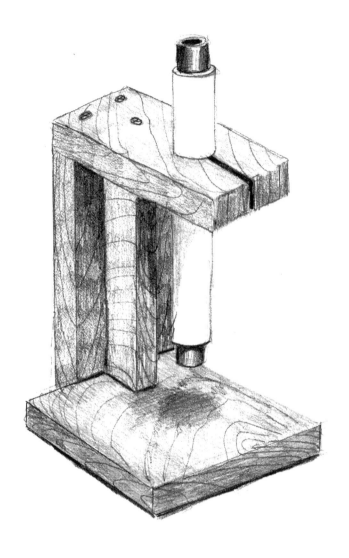

This microscope makes a great
field microscope. Just slide it
out of the base and take it with
you on your next nature hike.

1

Homemade Microscope

In the old days, scientists had to make their own equipment, since there was no factory-made equipment. Today's young scientists should be encouraged to try making the equipment they need also. It is a fun way to learn how scientific tools work and it is good practice for when they need a tool that doesn't exist. A homemade microscope is a good place to start.

A good microscope is a wonderful way to introduce a child to the wonders of the natural world. But good microscopes tend to be expensive, costing many hundreds of dollars. By eliminating the fancy focusing equipment and housing, and spending most of your money for good lenses, a homemade microscope of good quality can be made for under $100.00.

Materials:

- part A: pine - 5" x 2 ½" x 3/4"
- part B: plywood - 5" x 5" x 1/2"
- part C: pine - 4.5" x 1½" x 3/4"
- part D: pine - 5" x 2½" x 3/4"
- part E: 3/4" PVC pipe 160mm (6.3") long
  (purchased at plumbing supply stores)
- 6 wood screws 6 x 1¼"
- 10X eyepiece*
- 4X (or 10X) objective lens*

*Look for eyepieces and objective lenses at scientific supply companies. One company, Connecticut Valley Biological Supply Company, http ://connecticutvalleybiological.com sells these lenses. The following prices are current for 12/2012.

Brock objective 10X $28.00

Brock 10X eyepiece $28.00

What to Do:

To make the microscope's body

1. Cut out parts according to parts list.
2. Drill a $1^1/_{16}$" hole in part A to hold PVC barrel of microscope.
3. Drill 6 screw holes in part A and part D as shown on diagram. These holes should be slightly larger in diameter than the screws.
4. Screw the microscope's body together.

To make the microscope's barrel

1. Cut the PVC pipe to 160 mm (6.3"). Microscope lenses are designed to work at this distance apart.

2. Ream out one end of the microscope barrel with a 15/16" drill. If this is done carefully with a drill press, the eyepiece will fit snugly into the microscope barrel.

3. Place the objective lens in the other end of the microscope barrel. Depending on the PVC pipe, the objective lens might fit very loosely, in which case the lens must be taped in place. Or it might not fit at all; in which case, the PVC pipe will have to be reamed out so the eyepiece fits. Then tape the eyepiece in place.

4. Place the microscope barrel in the hole you cut in part A. It should fit snugly enough so that the microscope barrel can be raised and lowered by twisting and pushing it up or down. If the hole is too large, place a small piece of paper between the wood and the microscope barrel.

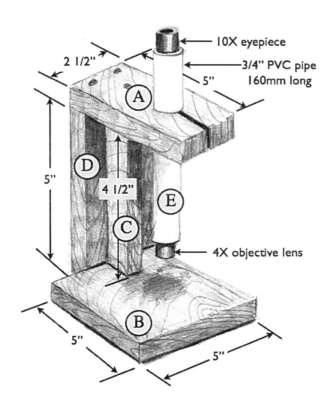

Try using your berlese funnel in
different habitats and at different
times of the year.

2

Berlese Funnel

As you walk through the woods, look down. What are you standing on? Unless you are on a well-worn path, chances you are standing on leaf litter – decomposing leaves, twigs and conifer needles. If you are like most people, you have probably never given the leaf litter a second thought while walking through the woods looking for wildlife. And yet, in many forests, the leaf litter houses the largest concentration of animals of any place in that forest.

The leaf litter creates the perfect environment for many small creatures. Because the litter acts as insulation, temperatures are much more stable under the litter than above it. The litter also acts as a moisture trap, staying moist through the hottest part of the day. Because of these conditions, a square foot of leaf litter may be home to thousands of mites, spiders, springtails and insects. One way that scientists collect these creatures is with a berlese funnel. Berlese funnels are simple to make and easy to use.

Materials:

- one gallon plastic milk bottle
- a collecting bottle – any small jar with a tight fitting lid will work
- a piece of screen that will fit inside the milk bottle
- a stick

- tape
- rubbing alcohol
- a lamp with an incandescent bulb

What to Do:

1. Cut the bottom off the milk bottle.
2. Turn the milk bottle upside down and place it in the jar.
3. Tape the stick to the milk bottle and the jar to hold the milk bottle in place.
4. Fold the screen so it fits inside the milk bottle. The screen will be used to hold the leaf litter in the milk bottle – so the litter doesn't fall through the bottle into the jar.
5. Cut a few small holes in the screen so larger animals can fall through.
6. Place some leaf litter in the milk bottle.
7. Turn on the light and place it over the milk bottle.

As the heat from the light dries out the leaf litter, the animals will crawl down the litter to stay in the moist area. Eventually, after a few days, as the leaf litter dries completely, the animals will be forced through the screen and will fall into the jar.

You can then observe the animals that have fallen into the jar with a hand lens or a dissecting scope.

If you want to preserve the animals, then you can put a little rubbing alcohol into the jar when you set up your funnel. When the animals fall into the alcohol they will be killed. Put the lid on the jar and the animals will be preserved indefinitely.

This activity was adapted from directions by:
John Meyer
Department of Entomology, NC State University
http://www.cals.ncsu.edu/course/ent591k/berlese.html

This space reserved for
Nature Drawings
from my backyard

Follow the color changes of the leaves in the fall by doing a series of chromatographs over a period of time.

3

Hidden Colors

Chromatography is a technique used to separate chemicals by color. As the chemicals travel through paper by capillary action*, some of them move faster than others. If the chemicals are colored, distinct colored bands will show up on the paper.

Chromatography is a tool used by many scientists to identify chemicals in a sample. This technique is often used in crime labs.

In this chapter, you will find two chromatography activities. The first one will display the ink colors in a "washable" black marker and the second will reveal the hidden colors in a leaf (see the nature story, "Mother Nature's Fashion Show" pg. 23).

*capillary action is described as the tendency of liquids to move through small tubes and air-like openings that are found in porous materials. This happens because the molecules of the liquids are more attracted to the walls of the openings than to each other.

Find the Colors in black ink

Materials:

- variety of water soluble "washable" felt tip black pens
- strips of paper towels or white coffee filters
- paper or plastic cup
- pencil
- tape
- water

What to Do:

1. Tape one end of the paper strip to the pencil as shown.
2. Draw a line with the marker an inch or two from the bottom of the paper strip.
3. Balance the pencil on top of the cup as shown.
4. Pour water into the cup so that the bottom of the paper strip is in the water, but the marker line is just above the water.
5. Watch over the next 15-45 minutes as capillary action draws the water up through the marker line and separates out the hidden pigments. Heavier pigments separate out first, lighter ones will separate out further up the piece of paper.

Hidden Colors in a Leaf

This activity should be done under adult supervision since it uses rubbing alcohol instead of water.

The green we see in plant leaves is the pigment chlorophyll. Stored in the cytoplasm of plant cells, it is responsible for creating food for the plants. Chlorophyll uses the sun's energy to split water molecules and re-combine them with carbon dioxide in the air to make sugars. It's amazing to think that most of the mass of a big tree is created out of thin air!

The chlorophyll masks other pigments that are found in the leaves. Carotene (the orange in carrots) and xanthophyll (yellows) are usually present in the leaves, but are not revealed to us until the chlorophyll begins to break down in the fall as the tree begins to get ready for the winter. These pigments assist the chlorophyll in photosynthesis, utilizing some of the sunlight not used by chlorophyll. Another pigment is produced by some trees as the nights lengthen and become cooler. It is called anthocyanin (red/purples found in rose petals). It produces vivid red Fall colors. Some of these pigments are also visible in very early spring leaves, before the chlorophyll is produced. Anthocyanins can be seen all year long in leaves of plants such as Copper Beaches and Japanese Maples. What about brown Oak leaves? Other materials in plants can change the tint of the colors we see. Tannins (the brown in "tea") combine with the other pigments in Oak leaves.

Temperature, moisture content, soils, pH and other environmental factors can influence leaf colors as well.

Materials:

- green leaves
- strips of paper towels or white coffee filters
- plastic cup
- pencil
- tape
- rubbing alcohol (chlorophyll does not dissolve in water so alcohol must be used in its place).
- pan with hot water

What to Do:

1. Grind or snip the leaves into small pieces and cover with alcohol.

2. Place the cup with leaves and alcohol in the pan of hot water and let sit for 15 minutes.

3. Dip the edge of a fresh paper strip into the alcohol and set up the strip as described on page 80. This chromatography will have to sit overnight.

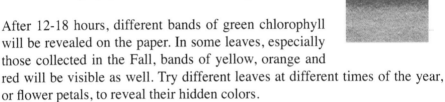

After 12-18 hours, different bands of green chlorophyll will be revealed on the paper. In some leaves, especially those collected in the Fall, bands of yellow, orange and red will be visible as well. Try different leaves at different times of the year, or flower petals, to reveal their hidden colors.

Thanks to Sue Stoessel at the Museum of Science in Boston for this activity.

This space reserved for
Nature Drawings
from my backyard

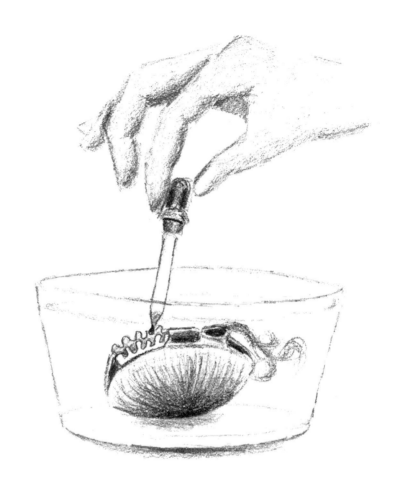

This activity works best on an
animal that has not fed for a
while. Collect your mollusk
that is left high and dry at low
tide.

4

Filter Feeders

Many mollusks, like clams, mussels, oysters and slipper shells, are filter feeders. They feed on the tiny planktonic plants and animals that live in the water. The water is taken into the body and passed over the gills. Tiny hairs on the gills separate the plankton from the water and pass it conveyer-belt fashion to the mouth. The water is expelled from the body. In areas with a lot of filter feeders, an amazing amount of water can be filtered in this way.

In many bivalves – mollusks with two shells like clams and mussels - the water is drawn into the body through an inhalant siphon and leaves the body through an exhalant siphon. These siphons are usually quite visible when the animal is feeding.

In filter feeding gastropods – mollusks with one shell like the slipper shell – there are no siphons. Instead, the shell is held tightly to the substrate except for a gap on each side of the font of the shell. Water enters through the gap on the left and leaves through the gap on the right.

In both cases, it is possible to watch the animal feed. You can do this experiment with freshwater or saltwater filter feeders. It can be done in the animal's natural environment or in a closed container such as a bucket or aquarium.

Materials:

- eyedropper
- food coloring
- bucket or small aquarium (optional)

What to Do:

If the animal you are testing is living in moving water – a stream or ocean with waves - the results of the experiment will be easier to see if the animal is collected and placed in a bucket or aquarium and covered with water (fresh or salt water depending on the animal). In this case, let the animal sit undisturbed in the water for a while to allow it to acclimate and start feeding.

If you are testing a bivalve, locate the inhalant and exhaling siphons. In many bivalves, these will be side by side.

Many bivalves, like clams and freshwater mussels may be completely buried in the substrate with just their siphons exposed to the water. Other bivalves like oysters and some mussels may not be buried at all. The experiment will work either way.

Using an eyedropper, place one drop of food coloring just in front of the siphons. If the mollusk is feeding, you should see the food coloring enter one siphon and exit the other.

If you are testing a gastropod like the slipper shell, locate the front of the animal. Look for a gap or two between the shell and the substrate.

Place one drop of food coloring just in front of the shell. If the animal is feeding, you should see the food coloring enter one side of the animal and exit the other.

Make sure you only use one drop of food coloring. If you use more, it may turn all the water blue and it may be hard to notice which way the water is moving.

This space reserved for
Nature Drawings
from my backyard

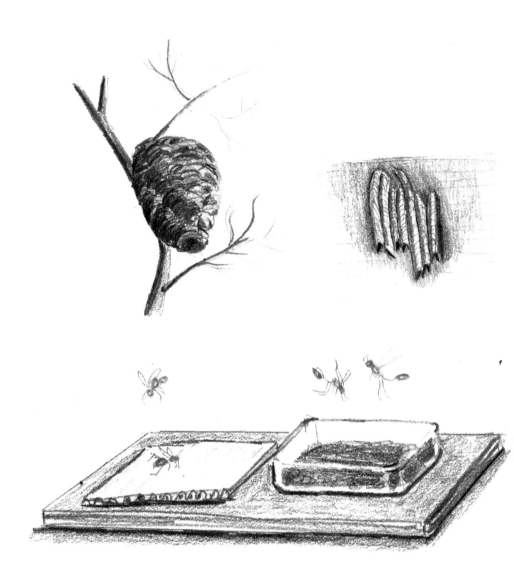

By following the wasps when they leave your feeder, you can locate their nests and watch them build.

5

Wasp Feeders

Most people I know are deathly afraid of wasps.

When a wasp approaches, they imagine the only thing on the wasp's mind is to sting. So they would no more encourage the wasp to build a nest nearby than they would encourage briars to grow over their favorite lawn chair. However, in this activity, that is exactly what I am encouraging.

Wasps can be divided into two groups – social wasps and solitary wasps.

Social wasps like the hornets and paper wasps build communal nests made of paper that may house a few to many hundreds of wasps, and they are very protective of these nests. They will defend their nest against any perceived threat. Anyone who has inadvertently stumbled upon one of these nests can attest to this fact.

Away from their nests, however, these wasps are much less aggressive. In fact, in order to get stung, you pretty much have to grab them and give them a squeeze.

Solitary wasps do not live in groups and do not build communal nests. They construct a nest, provision it with food, lay an egg and move on to build another nest. Since they leave the nest once they have laid an egg in it, they do not defend the nest. In order to get stung by a solitary wasp, you pretty much have to grab it and give it a squeeze.

Wasps are a gardener's friends.

Spend some time around flowers in the summer and you will see bees feeding on the nectar. As we all know, the bees are not only feeding, but also pollinating the flowers. You will also see wasps and hornets of many types feeding at the flowers. And just like the bees, they too are pollinating the flowers. They may not be the great pollinators that bees are, but these days, with bee populations plummeting, every bit helps.

Unlike bees, wasps are omnivorous. Not only will they feed on nectar and fruit juices, they also eat many insects such as flies, mosquitoes, aphids, gnats, cutworms and spiders.

So if wasps are actually beneficial insects, what can we do to encourage them? Well, we can supply them with nesting materials. And by placing these nest materials just outside our window, we can observe them, just as we do the birds at our window feeders.

These "Wasp Feeders" are easy to construct and just as easy to maintain. But best of all, unlike birdseed, these materials are free.

Hornets and paper wasps make their nests out of paper. Normally, they scrape pieces of bark from a tree to make their paper. But they are just as happy to use cardboard.

Many solitary wasps use mud to construct their nests. Homemade mud pies are just as appealing to them as the mud from a puddle.

Materials:

- board
- cardboard
- galvanized roofing nails (actually, any kind of nail or staple will work)
- 1 tupperware container
- mud
- water

What to Do:

1. Cover half the board with cardboard. Attach to the board with the roofing nails.
2. Attach the Tupperware container to the other half of the board. Use the roofing nails for this as well.
3. Fill the Tupperware container with mud. As the mud dries out, keep moistening it with water.

4. Moisten the cardboard with water to make it easier for the wasps to collect. However, you might want to moisten only half of the cardboard to see if the wasps prefer wet or dry cardboard.

5. Place the board on a table under your favorite window and watch the wasps "feeding".

When leaves decay, they generate heat.
The faster they decay, the more heat is
generated.
Try placing your thermometer in the
middle of a compost pile where there is a
lot of decay happening.

6

Winter in the Leaf Litter

If you are like most people, you accept long-held scientific beliefs. Especially those that are written in textbooks and taught in science classes. However, just because those beliefs are accepted by scientists doesn't mean you can't challenge them, or at least verify them. In fact, a good scientist is encouraged to do just that. In the process, you just might learn something new, something as yet undiscovered.

One scientific belief that I had learned in class long ago was that leaf litter was a good insulator. In our New England winters, finding a warm environment is essential for the survival of small creatures such as insects and spiders. Sometimes, a spot just a few degrees warmer can be the difference between life and death. Underneath the leaf litter, according to my textbook, was just such a place.

While I had learned about the insulating properties of leaf litter long ago, I finally decided to test it for myself.

Materials:

- two thermometers

When choosing thermometers to use, make sure you choose thermometers that:

- cover the temperature range you expect to encounter during your experiment.
- are waterproof or can fit in a waterproof housing.
- can be placed easily under the leaf litter.
- are calibrated so they read the same temperature. If they don't, (eg. if one thermometer reads 75°F while the other reads 72°F) subtract the temperature of the thermometer with the lower reading from the one with the higher reading. Every time you take a reading, add this number to the thermometer that had the lower reading.

What to Do:

1. Choose a place where the leaf litter is fairly thick – a few inches if possible.
2. Place the end of one thermometer below the leaf litter. If possible, place the thermometer in such a way that you can read the temperature while it is in place. If this is not possible, you can cover the whole thermometer with the leaves and uncover it when you need to read it but it will be easier if you can read the thermometer without removing it from the leaf litter each time.
3. Place the other thermometer so its end is just above the leaf litter.
4. Record the temperature from both thermometers.
   Take readings over the course of the winter and graph your results.

The graph below shows the results of my experiment from 2008. The dotted line shows the temperature under the leaf litter and the solid line the air temperature.

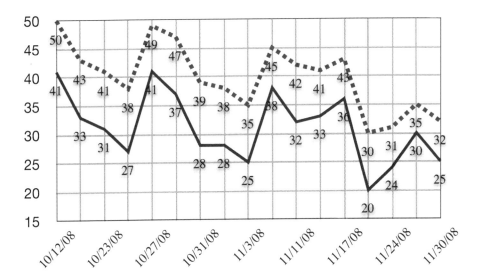

It doesn't matter when or how often you take your readings. In this experiment, you just want to compare the temperature below and above the leaf litter.

Further explorations:

Effects of shade

Try this experiment in a shady area and a sunny area. Take two sets of readings, one in the day and one in the night. What difference do you notice between the two areas?

Effects of rain

Each time you take a reading, record the amount of rain in the last twenty-four hours. Then compare the difference in temperatures on dry days to that on wet days. Does rain affect the insulative properties of the leaf litter?

Effects of snow

Place a third thermometer at a height above the highest expected snowfall. Now you have three temperatures to compare – leaf litter, ground level and air temperature. If there is snow on the ground when you take your temperature, record the level of snow over the thermometer. Is the temperature under the snow warmer or colder than the air temperature?

Obviously, reading the thermometers under the snow presents a problem. To do this experiment, I use a wireless indoor/outdoor thermometer. The outdoor thermometer has a temperature sensor at the end of a ten foot cable. I place three of these sensors in a housing to keep them dry– I use a lady beetle house but any box will work– and run the cables to where I want to take the temperatures. These thermometers transmit their readings to the indoor receiver where I can read the temperatures from the comfort of home. I don't even have to go outside to do this experiment.

This space reserved for
Nature Drawings
from my backyard

I tacked some leaves to the side of
my house, where they have dried out
in the sun. After 5 years, they are
still there, showing no signs of decay.

7

Leaf Decay

S tand in the woods in the fall for any length of time and you are sure to see a leaf fall from a tree. In fact, you will see lots of leaves fall. In many back yards, people rake the leaves into piles, put them into bags and throw them out with the trash. But for all of you people who let them lie where they fell, what happens to them?

Well, as you probably know, they decay. This, of course, means that they are eaten by insects, fungi, bacteria and a whole host of other organisms. But do you know which types of leaves decay the fastest? Or what conditions are best for leaf decay? Here is an easy to-do experiment that will supply you with some of the answers.

Materials:

- a few boards
  Size is not important, but a 3/4 inch thick board about 12 inches long by 4 inches wide will do nicely.
- a staple gun
- leaves from different trees
  If possible, find leaves that are still green and in good condition.

What to Do:

1. Collect a number of leaves from the different types of trees in your back yard.

2. Try to make sure the leaves are all about the same size and in the same condition. This makes comparing them at the end of the experiment easier.

3. Divide the leaves up into sets with one of each type of leaf in a set. For example, in each set have one maple leaf, one oak leaf, one aspen leaf and so on.

4. Staple one set of leaves onto a board – side by side but not touching. Do this for as many sets as you want to test.
   In your Nature Journal, record which leaves you put on the board and the date you put them there.

5. Choose different habitats to place each set of leaves. By placing them in different habitats you can see which conditions cause leaves to decay faster. You might want to place one set in the deep forest where they are always in the shade. Another might be placed under a pile of leaves where it is constantly moist. A third set might be placed out in the open where it gets a lot of sun. A fourth set might be placed submerged in a stream or pond. Record the locations and conditions in your journal.

6. Check your leaf sets after a week. Do the leaves look different than they did at the start of the experiment? Have they been chewed on? Do you notice any sign of decay? Record your observations.

7. Replace the leaves in their original spots. Then check them again in a week. Continue to check them every week until they have completely decayed, recording your observations as you go.

Did one type of leaf decay slower than the others throughout all of your habitats? If so, why do you think this was the case? One possibility is that many trees have chemicals in their leaves that are distasteful to insects.

Perhaps these chemicals also are distasteful to the organisms that are causing the leaf decay. Next summer, check the leaves of the trees from your experiment.

Does the insect damage you see on the trees correlate with the leaf decay rates you saw in your experiment?

What conditions did you find most favorable to leaf decay? Did they decay faster in a moist or dry environment? Did the amount of sunlight they received make any difference? What other factors may have influenced leaf decay? Can you make an assumption why certain conditions caused the most rapid leaf decay? Can you come up with an experiment to test your assumption?

Even though we see the world in 3-D,
we are still fascinated by 3-D
pictures.

8

3-D Photography

People have always been fascinated by 3-D photography. Whether it's through the old fashioned View-Master we used as a kid, or the red-blue glasses we wear while watching a full-length feature film in a movie theater, there is something special about 3-D. Even though we see the world in 3-D every time we look at the real world, somehow it is not the same. So, in this activity, I will show you how you can make and enjoy your own 3-D photos. All you need is a camera - any camera, your computer and two toilet paper cardboard tubes.

How 3-D Works

Notice that our eyes are separated by a couple of inches. Yet when we look at something, our eyes do not look straight ahead. The left eye does not look at an object that is a couple inches to the left of what our right eye is looking at. Rather, they look at the same spot. They look at it from slightly different angles. They see two slightly different pictures. You can demonstrate this by turning a piece of paper on its side and writing numbers on the lines. Staple the paper into a cylinder and place it on the table so the numbers face you. Look at the paper with the left eye and notice the smallest number you can see. Then close the left eye and open the right eye. Do you see the same numbers?

 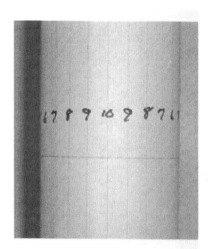

The brain receives these two different pictures and interprets them as a 3-D image.

If you look at an object with only one eye, you see it in two dimensions - like a picture on a book. When you see the world as a two dimension image, it is hard to judge distances, since everything seems flat. Nothing seems closer or further away than everything else. Here is another little experiment to demonstrate this point.

Close your eyes and have someone place one of your toilet paper tubes in front of you on a table at a distance you can reach.

Open one eye and try to touch the tube from the side. If you try to touch the tube from the front, you can just keep reaching until you touch the tube without having to judge the distance. If you try to touch it from the side and you judge the distance incorrectly, you will miss the tube.

Now open both eyes and try to touch the tube from the side.

Two eyes - two different pictures going to the brain - lets us see things in 3-D.

Make Your Own 3-D Pictures

Now that you understand how 3-D works, you are ready to have fun creating your own 3-D pictures. All you need to do is take 2 pictures of an object - each one at a slightly different angle. Then send one picture to your left eye and the other to your right eye. Your brain will do the rest.

What to Do:

1. Take a picture of the object of interest.

2. Move over about two inches and take the same picture. When you take the second picture, try to make sure the only difference in the two pictures is the two inches you moved over. If possible, place your camera on a flat surface, take the first picture, then slide the camera over two inches and take the second picture.

3. Print your pictures or download them onto your computer. Either way will work when it comes time to viewing your 3-D pictures.

4. Place the two pictures a little distance apart and look at them, using your two toilet paper tubes. The center of the pictures should be the same distance apart as the center of your two eyes. Hold one tube up to you left eye and the other to your right eye - as in the drawing on page 102. Point the left tube to the picture on the left and the right tube to the picture on the right - a couple of inches away from the pictures.

5. Normally, both of your eyes look at the same spot. Here, you are trying to get your eyes to look at two different spots - the two pictures separated by a couple of inches. If you relax your gaze a little, they should do this as they focus on the two pictures and the 3-D image should pop into view.

6. Another way to view the 3-D image is with a stereoscope. A stereoscope is a device that looks like a funny pair of glasses on a stand. One lens directs your left eye to the left picture and the other directs your right eye to the right picture. They are easier to use than the toilet paper tubes, but they do cost a little money.
    But if you have trouble making the toilet paper tubes work, you might try a stereoscope.

There are many parts of this activity that you can experiment with. Here are just a few. I am sure you can come up with many more:

- the distance you moved the camera for picture number two
- the size you print the pictures
- how far apart you place the images before looking at them (try placing the center of the pictures the same distance apart as your eyes)
- put the left picture on the right and the right picture on the left
- try taking the pictures through the lens of a dissecting microscope

Here are a few pictures that I took using the technique described above.

Azalea bud

Photo taken with FujiFilm 3.2 megapixel point and shoot camera

Firefly

Photo taken with Canon Rebel SLR with 50mm macro lens

Moss

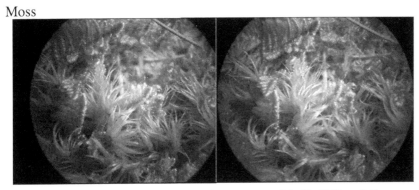

Photo taken through dissecting microscope with FujiFilm 3.2 megapixel point and shoot camera

Pine Trees

Photo taken with FujiFilm 3.2 megapixel point and shoot camera

I bring my whirligig eyes with me
when I go for a paddle on the
river. Every so often, I just lean
over the edge of the kayak and
take a look at what is below.

9

Whirligig Eyes

As I drift along the river in my kayak, I know that life is teaming in the water underneath me. Dragonfly larva wait in ambush for some unsuspecting prey. Clams lie half buried, sucking in water for their daily meal of plankton. Baby eels are slithering their way between the rocks, making their way upstream. Snapping turtles are half hidden in the mud, ready to pounce on unsuspecting fish who are, in turn, waiting to pounce on smaller unsuspecting fish. I know this world exists but I just can't see it. Between the glare of the sun and the ripples on the water, my eyes are just not adapted to see this fascinating world below. Oh, if I only had the eyes of a whirligig beetle, with two sets of lenses - one in the air looking above and one in the water looking below.

Well, where nature has failed me, ingenuity must serve. I need to supply my own whirligig eyes - or underwater viewer. I can either buy one or make one. Of course, the easy way is to buy one. But the fun way is to build one. It doesn't matter what you use to build it - use whatever materials are at hand - but whatever materials you use, the principal is the same.

The uneven surface and reflective properties of the water prevents us from having a clear view of the underwater world, so we must eliminate the surface and enable our eyes to look below it.

Basically, we are creating a container with a clear bottom and open top. By holding the container half in the water so the clear bottom is under the surface and the open top is above the surface, we can eliminate the need to look through the surface.

The easiest, cheapest and least durable way to do this is to take a can and cut out both the top and bottom. Place a sandwich bag over the bottom and pull it tight. Try to get all the wrinkles out and make sure the opening of the bag does not go below the surface.

A more durable and much better viewer can be made from a plastic bucket and a piece of clear Plexiglas. Cut the bottom out of the bucket and glue the Plexiglas to the bottom ridge of the bucket, using silicone glue. This gives you a nice wide viewer that lets you explore the underwater world. A dark bucket works better than a light one. When you look in the bucket, you want the brightest thing you see to be the view through the clear plexi - not the light shining through the sides of the bucket.

This space reserved for
Nature Drawings
from my backyard

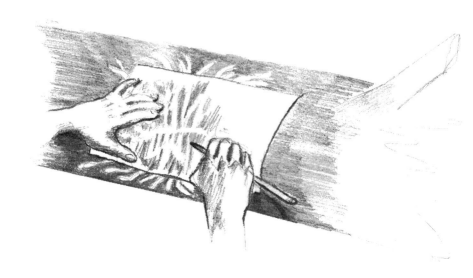

If you go hiking with young children, bring along a crayon and some paper. Having them look for good rubbing twigs will keep them engaged.

10

Bark Beetle Engravings

Have you ever seen a bark beetle? If so, you probably don't remember it. Most bark beetles are about the size of a grain of rice and are pretty nondescript. Not much to draw them to you attention.

Have you ever seen the tunnels of a bark beetle? If so, you probably do remember the patterns, even though you may not have known what caused them. If you are like me, you probably picked up the piece of wood with the tunnels and carried it around with you, thinking you might like to bring it home as a souvenir of your trip to the woods.

There are many different types of bark beetles and each one has a slightly different life history, but in general, it goes something like this: An adult bark beetle chews through the bark of a tree. In many instances, the tree, or the part of the tree the bark beetle is entering, is stressed or damaged.

The beetle excavates a tunnel or "gallery" in the space between the inner and outer bark, laying eggs as she goes. Once the eggs hatch, the young larva feed on the inner bark, leaving a trail as they go. These trails radiate out from the main gallery made by the adult female. Often, the effect of the whole gallery - adult and larval trails, is like a centipede carved into the wood.

The galleries remain hidden under the bark until the tree has died and the bark fallen off, exposing the galleries.

Occasionally, you might find the tunnels on a piece of wood too large to take home to include in your collection of nature treasures. Not to worry. You can easily make a rubbing of the tunnels and bring home the rubbings.

Materials

- wood with bark beetle galleries (look for wood that has had the bark removed or look under loose bark)
- paper
- crayons or soft-leaded pencil

What to Do:

1. Lay the paper flat on the wood over the bark beetle gallery (if the gallery is on a narrow branch, wrap the paper completely around the branch to hold it in place).

2. Rub the crayon or pencil on the paper over the bark beetle gallery. Press down hard enough so you get an impression of the gallery on the paper.

If you collect a number of rubbings of different galleries, you can make a Bark Beetle Rubbing scrapbook. Include as much information as possible about each rubbing - what kind of tree the rubbing was on, the diameter of the branch it was on, how high on the tree the galleries were on the tree and so forth. A little research on the internet might help you identify the genus or even the species of your bark beetle.

This space reserved for
Nature Drawings
from my backyard

Try covering the opening of the box with different colored filters. Do the plants react the same to different colors of light?

11

Plant Maze

I went outside the other day and sat down at our garden to watch the vegetables. Not surprising, they didn't seem to be moving. As we all know, most plants are rooted in the ground and can't move. Or can they? It all depends on how we define moving.

Most people would suggest that plants can't move because their roots hold them to one spot. But can they move their bodies while rooted in that one spot? We know that they move upwards as they grow, but can they control which way they grow? Think about it. If they could grow faster on the right side than the left, they will swerve to the left; and if they grow faster on the left side than the right, they will swerve to the right. Can they do this? Can they change directions if something is blocking their growing path?

As plants are growing up, sending out leaves, they are seeking the sunlight. The leaves need the energy from the sun for photosynthesis – to make their food. Here is a fun little experiment to see if plants can change the direction of their growth to reach the sun.

Materials:

- Pole bean seeds
- Potting soil
- Flower pot
- Cardboard
- Tape

What to Do:

1. Soak a few bean seeds in water for 24 hours.

2. Fill a small flowerpot with potting soil and plant the soaked seeds in the soil by pushing them under the soil by about ¼ inch.

3. Cut pieces of cardboard and tape them together to make a box. Only tape one side of the front of the box. This will be the hinge so the front can open up and you can access the inside of the box.
   The box in this picture is about 2 feet high by 1¼ foot wide by 4 inches deep. Your box only needs to be deep enough to fit your flowerpot in.

4. Cut a hole in the top of the box to let light in. The hole should be a couple of inches wide and can be in the middle of the top, or set off to one side.

5. Make two cardboard shelves inside the box – taping the shelves in place. Make sure the shelves are the same width as the box and that they completely block the path of the light from the hole in the top of the box to the planter. You don't want any light from the hole shining directly onto your plants.

6. Make sure that you cover all seams of your box so no light gets in the box except through the hole in the top. If you are using clear tape to make your box, you can cover up the seams by taping a piece of dark paper over them.

7. Place the flowerpot in the box, water your seeds, close the front door of the box and place the box in a sunny window so light enters the hole in the box. Or you can place your box under a lamp.

8. Every few days, open your box, water the seeds and observe how your plant is growing.

Be careful when watering the beans. Try not to spill the water onto the cardboard. For a more durable maze, coat the cardboard with a water based polyurethane and let dry before using.

After performing this experiment, try going outside to see if you can find any plants that have changed their growing direction. Try looking at the edge of a forest at small trees that may be shaded above by larger trees. Do you see any that are growing sideways towards the light instead of straight up?

Thanks to Lisa Warren at the Museum of Science in Boston for this activity.

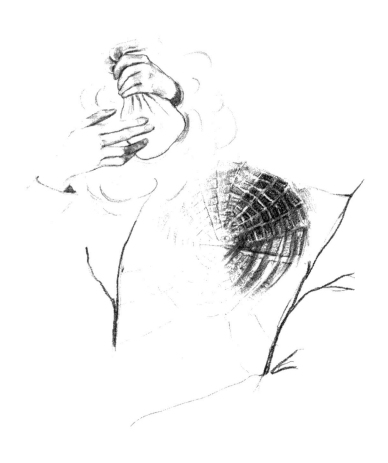

Dust an orbweb and each drop of
glue on the web will stand out.

12

Dusting for Spiderwebs

If you have spent much time walking through the woods, chances are at one time or another you have walked into a spider web. The threads of many spiders, especially small spiders, are so fine that they are almost invisible and will go unnoticed unless there is something sticking to it. That something could be an insect, dust or drops of water. For this reason, we notice many more spider webs on a cool moist morning when the dew coats everything including the spider webs. At these times, we may notice a web on the grass every few feet, while they will seem to disappear later in the day when the dew has evaporated.

I am always amazed to hear when people are surprised to learn that cobwebs are caused by spiders and not dust. Cobwebs are the webs made by a particular type of spider, namely cobweb spiders. They are basically invisible until they are coated with a fine layer of dust. If a coating of dust makes a cobweb visible, then it should make any web visible. So if you want to see the structure of a web, why not dust it?

This will not only allow you to see the web, it will also make it possible to photograph the web.

Spider webs come in a great variety including, cobwebs, sheet webs, orb webs, ray webs, funnel webs and many others. Dusting them brings out their unique structure.

Almost any book on spiders will have a section on their webs with accompanying diagrams. My favorite spider web diagrams are from the book, "How To Know the Spiders", a Pictured Key Nature Series book. It is out of print as far as I know, but used copies can be purchased from Amazon.

Materials:

- Cream of Wheat, flour or other very fine powder
- old sock

What to Do:

1. Find and old sock that doesn't have any obvious holes in it.
2. Fill the bottom third of the sock with flour or other fine powder. Tie off the sock right above the powder.
3. Find a spider web that you wish to dust. Hold the sock just upwind of the web and tap the sock lightly. The powder will come out of the sock and cover the web.

When I'm not using my sock, I keep it in a bread wrapper to prevent the dust from getting all over everything and to keep it dry.

before dusting

after dusting

Look for plants growing in the crack of a rock. As the plant grows, the crack will get wider - eventually breaking the rock in two. Now that is power!

13

Seed Power

In this experiment, you will use craft supplies and a
few dried beans to demonstrate that new plants, though
delicate, are capable of feats of enormous power.

A seed is the beginning of a plant. It is the result of a
reproductive process that begins with flower production and ends in
pollination, or the transfer of male pollen to the female ovule (or
egg). The end product is a seed: a plant embryo packaged in a protective
wrapper and enclosed with some stored food.

Seeds come in all shapes and sizes. Large as a coconut or small as a
grain of sand, they all contain stored energy that allows them to grow and
develop. Just where does this energy come from? The power of a seed is
locked in the oils, fats and carbohydrates (starches) that fuel its growth. With
this energy, the baby plant is able to germinate. Its cells awaken and expand,
exerting a force on the outside world.

In this way, tree roots lift and
break through concrete sidewalks,
weeds grow through paved roadways
and the roots of houseplants are able
to crack the pots in which they are
planted. In this experiment, bean
seeds use a combination of stored
energy and water pressure to burst
through (or in some cases lift off) the
plaster of paris in which they are
planted in.

Materials:

- plaster of paris
- bean seeds
- potting soil
- coffee can or cup

What to do:

1. Soak a few bean seeds in water for 24 hours.
2. Mix plaster of paris with water to a putty-like consistency (3 parts plaster of paris to 1 part water) and pour about one inch into a coffee can or cup.
3. Plant the seeds about 1/4 of an inch down by poking them into the plaster and smoothing over the top. Plant other seeds in soil and pour the plaster of paris on top.

NOTE: For faster results, soak the seeds for 48-72 hours. It is also a good idea to plant more than one seed in each cup, as even in the best of conditions, not all seeds grow.

The plaster will set in about a half hour. Seeds will probably not need watering. However, if the plaster is extremely dry after a few days, add water sparingly. Within a week or two, the seeds should break through the plaster.

Extending the Science:

- Try the same experiment with other seeds. Are some stronger than others? Set up an experiment to find out.

- Take a walk looking for things growing through cracks.

- At the beginning of a school day, fill a container (coffee can, jelly jar, anything with a snap-on plastic lid) with whole dried peas or bean seeds, to the very top. Fill the container with water (again, to the very top). Snap on the lid, cork or stopper. Wait six or eight hours, watch the swollen, growing seeds pop the top off.

Future Possibilities:

Discuss how people utilize plant power. We eat seeds, leaves, stems and roots for all types of foods - which in turn provide us with the energy to play hopscotch, do jumping jacks, (or our science homework...as the case may be.)

My thanks to Lisa Warren from the Museum of Science in Boston for this experiment.

Made in the USA
Charleston, SC
17 January 2013